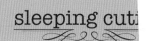

CAT NAPPING

A Cat's Guide To Slowing Down

David & Heidi Cuschieri

First Edition 2013

National Library of Australia
Cataloguing-in-Publication entry:

Cat Napping: A Cat's Guide To Slowing Down / David and Heidi Cuschieri

1st ed.
ISBN 9780987299314 (pbk.)

Sleeping Cuties series

Self-actualization (Psychology)
Inspiration.
Cats.

158.1

Published by The Next Big Think
Printed and bound in Hong Kong
For further information about orders:
Email: info@the-next-big-think.com
Website: www.the-next-big-think.com

CATS PROVIDE THE
GREATEST INSPIRATION
FOR LIVING.

How To Create Your Own Domestic Bliss

Cats are highly intelligent creatures. When cats were wild they would spend most of their time relaxing and cat napping, and when they were hungry they would for a short period summon the effort to catch their prey.

Cats are efficient hunters as they have ample time to work things out before doing anything. They are definitely enlightened beings not interested in doing. When humans 'domesticated' cats thousands of years ago I don't think they quite realised just how intelligent cats were. It didn't take long for cats to show humans who were really the 'domesticated' ones.

Have you ever seen a cat work hard? Cats didn't take long to transform human beings into human 'doings' at the beck and call of their feline masters. You may have heard the saying, 'Dogs have owners, cats have staff' - cats have all the time in the world because they have worked out how to become the master of the house. In fact, when humans first decided to 'domesticate' cats, cats had other plans. Cats became the masters of their new domain. Instead of becoming domesticated, these regal beings, with ease and grace, and without much more than lifting a paw, dominated all what their sleepy eyes surveyed.

So what are some of the lessons you can learn from cats? Firstly, that life is too short to rush around and you could do well to take a leaf out of a cat's book and slow right down. Cats subscribe to the 80/20 rule of life. 80% of the time is best spent taking it easy, and 20% instructing others to do as you please. All this ample time gives them the means to build up their intelligence.

Cats can also teach us that if we take time out regularly to rest and recuperate we will remain healthy and resilient, less stressed and ultimately a lot happier. We human beings can have nine lives too if we learn to spend more time 'being' in between all that 'doing' that we have become adept to.

Cats are the epitome of purrrfection. In ancient Egypt cats were worshipped as gods. They are graceful in the way they look and move, and luck seems to follow them simply because they have mastered the art of living. Nothing much has changed since ancient Egyptian times. Cats are still worshipped, yet it is time to start taking notes out of the book of cats - slow down, relax more and begin to live up to our birth right as human beings and not human doings. Cats hold the answers to experiencing our own lasting happiness if we only take the time to sit, relax, observe and learn from these purrfectly divine beings.

Decisions
always seem
easier
after a good
cat
nap.

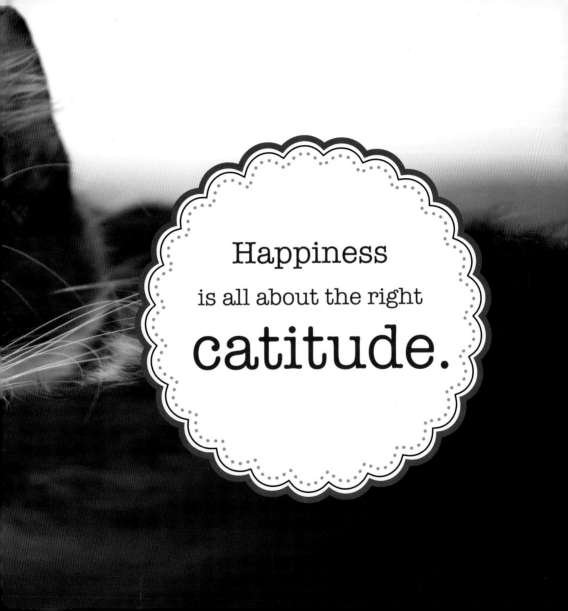

Happiness

is all about the right

catitude.

Ideas of sheer genius
are borne between the sheets.

I have never known a cat
who suffered from
insomnia.

The best cure for
grumpiness
is a good night's
sleep.

We all have exactly 24 hours in a day.
If you believe you have less time
than others to pause and relax,
it means you have different

PURRiorities.

There is a lot humans can learn from their feline companions.

The biggest lesson humans can learn is that a lot can be achieved with little effort when you put your mind to it.

Cats have
nine lives
to make up for the time
sleeping between
wakefulness.

Cats
invented
beauty
sleep.

To reach the
stars
firstly you need
to have your
head in the
clouds.

Sleeping is
simply
divine.

When you slow down

you will come to notice that it is

the little things

like the morning sun
and a summer breeze

that hold the magic to

happiness.

When you are
tired
sleep is a welcome
friend.

Why spend **nine lives** stressing.

That's why humans only have one life.

Television and sofas were invented as a cure for insomnia.

Put your **paws** in the **air** like you just don't **care.**

Whoever invented **blankets** must have been a **cat.**

Slow down
&
smell
the catnip.

We were told that PCs would revolutionise how we lived, worked and how we spent our leisure time. The problem is no one took notice.

Pussy Cats (PCs) have been with us for thousands of years sharing their knowledge and technology of how to really live.

Too much
stress
will make you
ill.

Too much
sleep
will make you
fat.

Balance
is the secret
to good
health.

A wise cat once said, 'he who lifts a paw had better have a darned good reason for it!'

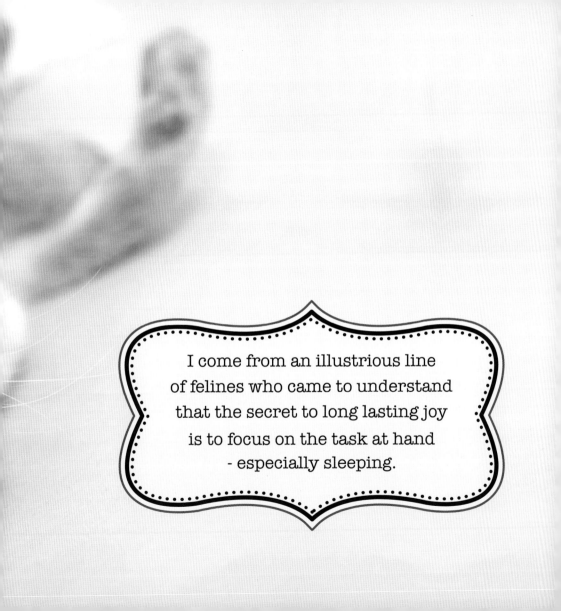

I come from an illustrious line
of felines who came to understand
that the secret to long lasting joy
is to focus on the task at hand
- especially sleeping.

A smile
makes every day
shine.

The best
exercise
is a good stretch
before and after
sleep.

Life
teaches us
that it is too short to
rush
through it.

We close our eyes when we

sleep

to see the

stars

in our dreams.

Do everything with
gracefulness.
Nothing in life
that is worth
doing
is worth
rushing.

The world is so

upside
down.

People live to

work

rather than work to

live.

· ·

Maybe its time to get your

purriorities

right.

· ·

Look after the
small
stuff like sleeping
and the big stuff has
an uncanny way of
sorting itself out.

Humans think cats
sleep a lot - we don't
we meditate.

Sleep is the
pastime of geniuses.
A good sleep helps you
think outside the

box.

Sofa

so good...

Quiet time is a time to reflect and appreciate

your pawsomeness.

Alarm clocks

were definitely not
invented by cats.

You simply cannot rush

purrfection...

Pillows are filled with
feathers
so that when we fall asleep our
dreams
can take
flight.

Cats understand that
great things
cannot be accomplished
without enough
sleep.

Pause
awhile.

Cats invented the

siesta.

It has only taken a
few hundred years
for a select few races
of people to perfect it.

Things often feel **pawsitive** after sleeping on it.

When sleep arrives
don't fight it.

Thank You

We have brought together our words and the images of others, to send out special messages to touch the hearts and lives of people the world over.

Thank you to all who have made this book possible - the people who have touched our lives so that we could write the words of wisdom that fill these pages; the photographers who's images give us joy and wonder; the printers for their attention to detail and assistance; the distributors for their guidance, passion and belief; the retailers for their support; and last but not least, to the gift givers and receivers who will pay it forward and carry on the essence of what our gift books are all about.

Share With Others

Life is a journey and along the way we are given sign posts.
At certain times we may not recognize these, but when we come back to this
spot, all of a sudden we see with our hearts not our eyes. This book is similar.
At different chapters in your life you will come back and leaf through this book
and all of a sudden the words will speak to you in a different way and help
you to see your life and experiences from a new perspective.

Words can transform lives and we would love to hear what impact this book
may have had on you or someone you have given this book to.

Your words can change others' lives in a way you never thought possible.

All of us have experiences that when put into words can inspire, bring joy and
hope to complete strangers, even if we may not think so.

Share your words with the world at: **www.my-happyness.com**

Happiness is something we
are not taught at school or at home.

And as such many of us fail to find
lasting happiness and fulfillment in our lives.

Happiness is a good habit to learn.

We will show you how easy it
really is to be happy, one day at a time.

Even if you think you are too busy to be happy.

Visit our website today.

www.theschoolofhappyness.com